SICGU DhargeyPublishing
Developing Our Candlelight-like Wisdom

The Book of How

By
Geshe Jampa Kunchog Pryor

© 2022 by Jampa Kunchog Pryor

All rights reserved. No part of this book may be reproduced, stored in a retrieval system or transmitted in any form or by any means without the prior written permission of the publisher except by a reviewer who may quote brief passages in a review to be printed in a newspaper, magazine or journal.

First Edition

ISBN 978-0-9990141-5-8

Edited by Susan Keillor

Design by Karma Mipham Wangmo

www.sicgu.org

Water always determines its path based on the force of gravity. Similarly, when following our path to the future, we must use our goals as gravity. In doing so, success will always be met, obstacles will be bypassed. The reality is that those who do not set goals are always confronted by recurring problems. Those who have objectives always find the proper solution.

$$S = (A+CF) > P$$

The solution equals the application of continuous force greater than the problem.

Contents

Introduction 1

Establishing Our Focus 3

Gaining Confidence and Overcoming Doubt 5

In Pursuit of Wisdom 7

Building a Template 9

The Way 11

Finding the Way 15

The Rules 21

Ideology 31

Avoidance of Strong, Exploitation of Weak 33

The Method 35

Why do We Need Theory 37

A Matter of Choice 39

Building Wealth 41

Insight Through Education 43

About the Author 45

About SICGU 47

About SICGU Dhargey Publishing 49

Introduction

As in war, so it is in peace. The condition of being in a state or war or in a state of peace is determined only by ourselves. Our world is no more than a projection of what we have decided it to be. Regardless of the decisions of others, how we maintain our world will develop the experience of peace or strife. Those without internal convictions will be the first to fall prey to the ambitions of others. Those who determine their world will live in an existence that they have sculpted.

The mental factors we experience are not more powerful than the decisions we choose to follow. The world is no greater than what we have decided it to be. The efforts we put forth determine what will be passed on to others. We have a great responsibility every day we live. The methods we use to determine our lives must be well contemplated.

The purpose of this writing is to illuminate the notion of our personal responsibility for developing internal growth and to discuss the power of our individual influence regarding the world we live in. When the accountability of changing the world confronts us, we can, and we must, face all obstacles and vanquish them through reasoning devoid of speculative belief. There is nothing that cannot be overcome. Only when we believe that we cannot achieve something, success becomes unachievable.

There should be no confusion regarding the relationship between our moral deeds and worldly responsibilities. If we do not identify the relationship between the two, our efforts will be only partially beneficial. Moral responsibilities guard us from transgressions against others, and knowledge of worldly activity helps us to form the borders of what we are willing to do.

If in dealing with the world around us we decide that we cannot do it anymore, our advancement stops, the potential of gaining further progress ends. The cause of this obstacle arises from the thought "I cannot do it," which comes from a personal feeling of inadequacy. This happens because of our lack of confidence in our own potential. The condition of doubt only exists because we have been taught to believe in a world of limitations. We defeat ourselves because of inherited beliefs. The reality is that the only limitations we have are the ones we believe in.

The ability to be victorious over such imagined boundaries is achieved by clearly understanding what correct learning is about. Capability belongs to the realm of learning – the more we strive towards learning, the deeper we set the foundation of insight and the more stability we find in our lives.

Establishing Our Focus

The distinction between the art of war and the art of peace should be discerned by the nature of our motivation.[1] This is not an art in the sense of creating a sensually stimulating experience, it is an art in its capability to craft opportunity through reason.

The reality of our transitional existence is that there will always be conflict, be it large or small. There will always be conditions of opposing forces. By recognizing this, we can understand the need to achieve an advantage when disadvantage appears. Obstacles are inevitable. When we wake up in the morning, we should be cognizant of the possibility that a conflict might arise. The reality of this world should not be based on what we believe it to be, but on what we can establish from it. Belief based on our emotional thoughts only distorts the reality of what we could know.

It is crucial that we answer the question why we should proceed with any endeavor or why we should not. In *The Light of Meditation,* we talk about hearing proper instructions and then contemplating on what we have heard. This is an essential step in decision making. In mastering techniques of hearing and contemplating the nature of the problem, we can resolve all challenges.

The initial step is to become acquitted with the problem at hand. We have to identify what has become an obstacle to us and why, then we can find resolution through the process of simplification. Simplification is the process of moving forward, avoiding the strong and exploiting the weak points. It implies focusing on one's goal, understanding what supports or obstructs it and leaving whatever is not pertinent to it aside. This is developed though understanding the instructions necessary to achieve success and then applying that understanding with strong faith.

By identifying the immediate problem at hand, we do not become distracted.[2] Distractions are often caused by assumptions, not validly examining the logical sequence of events. Identification of what we must do can be done by discerning if the consequences will be beneficial to us or not. If there is a benefit, proceed. If not, stop. We must actually see the benefit and not assume something to be good. When challenges arise, we have to answer these questions right; this will develop into a resolution.

---

1 More in the book *The Art of War and Peace.*

2 *The Light of Meditation,* also published by SICGU Dhargey Publishing, explains the Buddhist perspective on distractions in the chapter on the Mind and Mental Arisings.

Gaining Confidence
and Overcoming Doubt

Asking the correct questions regarding what we do not know is also a part of contemplation. If we understand that the present state of not knowing is only a temporary condition, we will start to understand that through the power of observation, we can develop extensive knowledge.

We must abandon fearful thoughts that cause us to think, "I am not capable of doing something" and replace them with an inquisitive mind, knowing that what is not understood now, will eventually become known. When examining realities surrounding us, we must not think there are things that we are not able to comprehend.

There are no paradoxes in life. Paradoxes only spring forth through misinterpretations or speculative beliefs based on the idea of personal limitations. There are temporary restrictions, of course, but like with anything short-lived, the time of limitations can be overcome. Those who excel in life, live under the belief of "I can"; those who do not, believe in "I cannot."

When we find ourselves wedged between two opposing beliefs, we can be overcome by doubt. Doubt is a divided mind that deceives us into not being able to be resolute about what we should do. Because of this mind, uncertainty arises, and judgements become weakened.

It is important to keep in mind that we do not have to be one hundred percent correct in all our decisions, what we need to be is correct. We are all apprentices at some time in our life. If we are brave enough to seek ways to overcome mistakes, we can become smart enough to develop templates to direct our actions. If our confidence is overcome by self-doubt, our decision making will constantly have to rely on someone else's interpretations to decide what we must do next. Because of indecision, our lives will be determined by another's point of view, and we will continue to be subservient to all types of assumptions.

To gain self-confidence, we have a long road to travel, but the more we participate in being confident, the more confident we become. The question we should ask ourselves now is how to proceed forward. The answer should be by the power of our investigations. Having the capability of answering any question depends on our own personal research. How much we have educated ourselves regarding our doubts and uncertainties will determine the level of success we will experience. The wise contemplator realizes that time and continuous effort are the methods of overcoming any obstacle.

In Pursuit of Wisdom

Abandoning unrealistic expectations is essential. Isolating ourselves from an imagined achievement of grandeur will assist us in proceeding towards our goals. What is certain is that with consistent effort, our goals will be achieved. Confidence grows through knowledge, and knowledge eliminates doubt.

Wisdom does not come from biological factors or a special sequence of genes. Wisdom arises from expansion of knowledge regarding what can be established as a reality. Insight comes from investigation and understanding grows from elimination of speculative acceptance of what we believe to be facts. We cannot rush to wisdom; it emerges through repetitious pursuit of understanding. Therefore, insight comes in increments.

The great Indian scholar Shantideva stated, "There is nothing that doesn't become easier through our repetition." If it takes us a hundred times to read and contemplate what we do not understand now, once we understand this topic, the knowledge is ours. The secret of understanding how to learn is in the time we must allot ourselves to achieve it. We cannot learn faster than what we are able to. Learning requires meticulous attention to detail. It is not about the quantity of information gathered; it is about the quality of understanding we are able to cultivate.

There is no rush, there should only be consistency. The statement that "there is nothing that does not become easier through repetition" reflects consistent familiarization with a particular subject. "Becoming easier" reflects the requirement of seeing something repeatedly. If we are learning something today, we should be able to measure our progress from year to year. This is done by marking our level of understanding when we first began. As time proceeds, we will see that we have gained deeper insight.

Building a Template

We are describing the groundwork of what we need to build upon. We must have a template to establish the direction we wish to journey. Templates lessen the obstacles of distractions by keeping us aware of the borderlines we must travel within. Distractions can be overwhelming, and they can become obstacles to what we wish to achieve. Successful outcome of our efforts depends on creating a template which we can use as a guide for our growth.

Planning is the fortress protecting our progress. Why do we need to plan? It establishes a direction as well as the reason behind why we are doing what we are attempting to do. By using our time of preparation, we will understand better how to deal with problems if we become confused regarding what we must do.

Plans establish the foundation from which our future growth will arise. For example, to build a strong house, we must construct the foundation of the envisioned building. The shape of the house depends on the structural basis we decided to use.

Having a template reminds us of the rules we must follow to achieve our ambitions. Guidelines formulate the fundamental conditions which will direct us towards our goals. If we are ordained, this can be seen in the vows taken. If we are entrepreneurs or builders, it can be seen in the usage of mathematics, and if we are doctors, it can be seen in the knowledge of anatomy and so forth.

This mode is the basis for educating ourselves more profoundly. If we venture forwards without a plan and an established reason for why we are doing what we are doing, our direction will become unclear. When unforeseen factors or difficult situations appear and we don't have a plan, we will have no answer, our thoughts will be limited to superficial doubts or a belief that we might not be able to succeed. To believe that we cannot do something is merely a projected belief. When the proper tools of accomplishment are understood, we begin to understand the power of confidence.

Luck has nothing to do with achievement. If we believe it does, we will grow feeble in the confidence we need to make the right decisions. Without a notion of a plan and without meeting people with insight into the necessary training, we will not achieve our goal. The lack of planning only ushers in a time of self-doubt. Not following rules assigns our future to chance or luck. This is a recipe for ruin. Those who believe that rules do not matter only sacrifice themselves to consequences they may not be prepared for.

Similarly to the saying of throwing good money after bad, success cannot be achieved by investing in more bad decisions. Bad decisions lead us into further troubles. This will not only harm ourselves, but may also harm those around us.

The Way

The Way is not the path, it is the method of achieving the path. It is our practice in conformity with the principles of the eight-fold path.[3] It is strengthened by our taking responsibility under the umbrella of compassionate determination.

It is essential to understand for all wishing to be a force of change that by the power of consistent effort and knowledge no obstacles can endure.

$$S = (A + CF) > P$$

Solution equals the application of continuous force greater than the problem.

The world is in constant transition. Our insight must reveal a different method for resolving each problem by creating alternative strategies to meet our challenges. Stagnant and inflexible rules can be outflanked by introspective tactics. Of course, initially we may not be as effective as we might wish to be, but this should be of no consequence to us. This is because our goal should be invested in a long-term outcome. Short-term gain should never be considered as an indication of our success. If we have short-term success, then take it. However, never forget the importance of long-term planning.

We need to be able to evaluate our progress and fortunately, there are methods of doing so. We must evaluate our expectations of accomplishment by measuring them on a scale of zero to one hundred percent. The assessment should take into consideration our planning, challenges, commitment, and the probability of a positive outcome. Our level of successful planning must be greater than any level of probability. The degree of chance should be understood as a condition of less than a fifty percent of probability of success. Chance is a guessing game approach to accomplishment and has no place for serious consideration.

When we understand that there is a possibility of attaining something, we can conclude that there is a method by which something can be attained. Therefore, the appraisal of our efforts should not be based on if something is possible or not, it must be based on the consideration if our actions are conducive to achieving those aspirations. We are dealing with a cause-and-effect scenario.

It is important to adhere to a percentage-based plan to scale the success of our efforts. This will help us to gauge our forward progress. Whatever our project may be, we should attempt to have a 51% or greater measurement to

---

[3] Eight-fold path: right view, right intention, right speech, right conduct, right livelihood, right effort, right mindfulness, right concentration.

success. However, 51% is not satisfactory, we must always strive for greater success.

When dealing with any situations of uncertainty regarding what you should or shouldn't do, ask yourself, what benefit does it bring to me? If you don't see a benefit, stop. Do not proceed. Uncertainty does not grasp what will bring accomplishment. Decision making should never rely on chance. The probability of a good outcome will most likely reap little to no advantage. If there is a gain, we will not understand how to reproduce it again. Our future should never be likened to the toss of the dice.

Our decision making should never be rushed. We should never be restricted by short-term deadlines. There should never be time restraints connected to what we must do. If we are told something must be decided now or we will lose out, walk away, we will at least leave with what we came with. If we don't make efforts to protect ourselves, what is ours now will be theirs later.

Never allow someone else to define your needs and never allow yourself to become a servant to your wants. Making our decisions from a stable and informed platform of rationality allows us to make correct decisions. Our lives have no time for mistakes and missed opportunity.

We will suffer loss of self-esteem and confidence if we don't find discipline in our thinking. Without discipline there will be no true self-confidence. There are people without discipline who have success but, their self-evaluation is built on imagined self-importance. This is not good.

Having a kind heart is the mark of superior thinking. Having a kind heart coupled with insight is power. If someone is attempting to force us into making split-second decisions, this should be seen as their attempt at profiteering. There is nothing that must be done now without having an opportunity to think.

In *The Art of War and Peace*[4] it states that prior to all engagements a general spends a long time in his temple contemplating all conditions prior to engagement. This passage illustrates the stipulation of gathering information and considering its validity prior to any engagement. This is so essential. Success is built on having the appropriate information at a suitable time. If we indulge in chance and speculation, we will never understand why some people are successful and why others are not.

Once we have comprehended what it means to know ourselves, then we must endeavor to know others. The art of knowing others should be comprehended as having the ability to understand someone else's intentions

---

4 *The Art of War and Peace* by Geshe Jampa Kunchog Pryor is the second part of this trilogy, *The Book of How* is its first part, while *The Way* is the third part.

or dedications. Because we know the reasons why we are doing something, when others don't assign to themselves the same interest, this indicates a possible conflict of intent. Our dedication should be centered around the group or goals we have established as being important. We must lean heavily on our own investigation and not compromise to what others may suggest we should do.

This is stated because as we have previously said, the general prior to all engagements spends a long time in his temple contemplating all conditions prior to engagement. Either we will have confidence in ourselves or not. If we know ourselves but do not comprehend the nature of others, our success will be only fifty percent accurate. We will lose just as much as we win. The odds will teeter on the notion of maybe yes or maybe not.

As we are driven by our intention to succeed, so are others. We should never fault anyone else for ambitions they display in their lives. In dealing with others, we must evaluate how much of a benefit they will bring to us before employing their help. When dealing with information, make sure that it is credible. Do you know its source? If you do not, show suspicion. Always ask why. Knowing others is essential. Life is a lesson on rules, we should never subjugate our future to chance.

The root of lasting success comes from the strength of bonding we develop between ourselves and others. There must be a balance between our ambitions and how our actions may affect or influence others. We must be aware of our own capabilities as being something real.

When we are able to combine our efforts with the united force of others, our collective capabilities multiply in intensity. If, for example, in trying to sweep a room we use only one straw, it would take us forever to complete a job. On the other hand, when a straw is bundled together with many others, the job quickly becomes completed.

This is the method of force multiplication. When there is a convergence of many different streams into one, a mighty river can be formed. In dealing with others, an agreement to have a uniting belief to a goal is essential. This means that everybody involved must be prepared to focus on what will bring about a victorious result.

Leadership must be able to inspire the willingness to do so. When introduced to a well-ordered governing body, dedication will follow. Do not merely direct your attention to people possessing credentials, if the well-educated people have no dedication to the organization or have disregard for rules, success will be impaired. On the other hand, people dedicated to an association can be trained to do anything.

The method of discerning potential can be judged through observation. We must steer our minds in the direction of understanding intention.

Appraise what are others are saying and why. When caution becomes a variable in our decision making, we will begin to understand more about the necessity of knowing others.

We are not saying not to trust in anyone, we are saying, always proceed forward based on our own understandings and use caution. Sometimes our emotions expose our vulnerabilities. In the pursuit of success, unknown situations can arise. Because of not seriously evaluating what we understand now, we could forfeit our dreams to people who have unrelated intentions.

The reality is that once we lose what we have, no one will share our suffering. We will be scorned and told we should have known better. The truth really is that we should have known better.

The only thing we should be fully committed to is the pursuit of our goal. Remember, this is what we have planned for and reflects who we are. This type of dedication is a contributing cause to being able to proceed forward.

There are many who will stop at nothing to get what is ours, and there are those who will react to us out of jealousy. This is a clear indication of their own weaknesses. We should understand that whatever others may project about us has nothing to do with who we are. When we understand their beliefs, we know who they are. At that time, we will understand what we must do.

We are not here to manipulate others, we are here to ensure our actions have no fault. The rule we must learn to be aware of in planning is to exploit the weakness and avoid what is strong.

Finding the Way

If our philosophical beliefs do not amount to something that brings us happiness, we should change our beliefs for something else. We should never underestimate the positive results we generate through the I-can-do-it attitude. As mentioned before, we must never underestimate our capabilities. We must keep in mind the thought that all we have to do is to find the Way. The gravity of our conviction will find the proper route to our objectives. This is because our desire to achieve becomes a continuous force greater than the problem that we face. The moment we stop is the moment our capabilities end.

We must always start our journey with the resources we have now, and not fantasize about having a better situation or engaging in it only if the conditions were different. The best we have is what we bring to the table now. All we need to do is to understand that with proper training, knowledge and determination, nothing can resist our efforts.

Knowing others is not for the purpose of mere competition for competition's sake. Knowing others is the process of determining strong and weak points in any relationship with the intention to adjust our efforts to face any transpiring challenge.

Simplification of a problem is the process of identifying exactly what the problem is. This capability comes through long thorough investigation, it comes through study, it comes through time. However, the more we engage in analytical thinking, the more our capabilities will improve. We should view ourselves as apprentices, then we will begin to understand that mistakes are possible, that is, only until we learn not to make them.

Do not fall back on your fears and indecisions. Even though doubts may arise in our lives, we should always rely on our training. We should have great faith in the laws governing cause, effect, and timing. When fears arise, ignore them. Ask yourself, does this problem fit within the realm of my training? Find the Way. For example, contemplate the nature of water. Water flows in conformity with the conditions it has to cross. When obstacles impede one direction, it follows its path of least resistance. It avoids the strong and exploits what is weak.

When a farmer plants his field in the spring, he does his work based on the knowledge of cause, effect, and timing. This action doesn't mean he must be one hundred percent correct about the outcome. This does not mean he might not have to adjust his work to changing situations. What he has to be is correct about is how to determine the outcome of problems as they might arise.

The outcome should always ensure at least fifty-one percent probability of success to be able to determine that we have not made a mistake. Of course, we should never be satisfied with such a low percentage, but this allows us to set realistic expectations. We shall remain flexible. Others might demand greater odds, but we must not be distracted by their lack of insight. Justify your reasons in clarity. There is never only one way of doing something. The correct way will be determined by the long-term outcome of our actions.

There are many levels of insight. This can be understood through the understanding that there are experts among experts, which means that levels of insight vary even among experts. There are some who understand the words but not the meaning, there are those who understand the meaning but not the words, those who understand both the words and their meanings and there are those who understand neither the words nor their meanings.

The advice here is to be tenacious in our investigation. The reality is that the one who spends more time contemplating the truth will understand more than those who don't. This has nothing to do with the level of intelligence a person has. It has everything to do with their desire to succeed. This goes for everything we endeavor to do.

My teacher Geshe Ngawang Dhargey once told me that when he started debating in Sera Jey University, he decided that he would go for a month-long retreat. When he returned, all his classmates knew more than he did. All we need to do is to be constant in our pursuit of knowledge. Knowledge we are talking about takes long term engagement instead of short-term planning.

Success is determined by our attitude and willingness to not give up. Our world will either grow or shrink in importance, based on our intentions to progress. During our progress, we must constantly adapt to internal and external conditions. Therefore, the notion of being internally flexible in our pursuit of our goals brings into the focus what is the real cause of success.

Once again, this brings into light the importance of informing ourselves. We should consider knowledge as something like a sponge that absorbs all water that contacts it. The only difference is that the capability of the mind is vast. When we underestimate the capability of our mind, we underestimate ourselves. To be extremely successful, we must always incorporate kindness in our intentions.

When our actions include a world greater than own personal benefits, we can greatly influence the minds of others. When we think about why we must remember others, we must contemplate that our very existence has depended on what they have done for us. We should never mistake our success as being devoid of their kindness. Within this though lies the importance of understanding how we must deal when interacting with others. Compassion is not an act of appeasement. Compassion is a mental arising that wishes others freedom from suffering.

Knowledge is the result of understanding what we seek to comprehend. Compassion allows us to take on the responsibility we owe to others. We can develop the foundation by practicing some simple rules. As His Holiness the Dalai Lama stated, "If you cannot do anything to benefit others, then at least refrain from doing anything to hurt them." This should be the guideline for our behavior, and it should embrace all our actions when dealing with others. We should never indulge ourselves in blaming someone else based on the belief that they have interfered in our progress. If sentient beings grasp happiness for themselves, we should not be angry.

There is not one way to achievements. What might work for one person might not work for another. We must engage in our actions based on our judgment, timing, and the changing conditions. We must determine our own actions and bear responsibility for what we do.

However, as stated previously, we must be educated and disciplined in the art of decision making and develop an insight into strong and weak points of a situation that faces us. This is the process of understanding what favors our success and what does not. When facing hindrances, forward progress is based on avoiding what is strong and taking advantage of what is weak. Remember the example of water, avoiding what is difficult by flowing in the direction that presents the least resistance to its forward progress. Therefore, even if the goal we seek is far into the future, we achieve what we need to achieve by simplification of the processes of advancement.

This method is an art. We gain insight through simplification of the problems we face. Of course, this is not intuitive, it is a process that is attained through long-term contemplation and attention to details. The enemy of insight is impatience. Advantageous things only happen when the conditions governing them are well understood.

Realistic understanding of our capabilities is essential. This is important to think about. In knowing our own abilities, we have the power to overcome personal weaknesses by identification of what these weaknesses might be. In most cases, the worst weakness we might have to face could be our own self-doubts. Insight only comes through extensive contemplation. Extensive contemplation comes through education.

Life is a marathon, and it offers no shortcut. Therefore, know yourself and work within your own comprehendible realities. Make decisions on the basis of what you understand and not on what someone else has advised you as being true. What we learn is just a measured scale of what might be feasible. It is our responsibility to test the validity of what we have been told. This is contemplation. Truth is established through the examination of the theories we hold. If our theories do not match reality, we must change our theory. If our efforts produce a situation that seems insurmountable, we should redirect our efforts in another direction that may reflect a more realistic path.

When working with a group of people, the method of building greater success is constructed by establishing a circle of dedicated people who will support the vision we have. An organization is only as good as the principal group of people we choose to represent our intentions. When such a group has been established, reaching the goal is just a matter of time.

Be careful to clearly explain to others the duties they are responsible for. Undisciplined actions, regardless of good intentions that we might be there, can evolve into unexpected results that bring conditions of doubt and disorder within a group. This can hinder our ability to progress or grow.

Life is a business that requires discipline to avoid unforced errors. Factors creating obstacles can appear in many ways. We must be aware of conditions that appear out of order or don't have the direction we intended. Our power of observation is essential. We must judge well our ability to work through obstacles or work around them. We must convince ourselves that no matter what the obstacles may be, they will never be a permanent fixture in our way.

Knowing ourselves goes far beyond the comfort line of just liking who we are. Knowing ourselves requires a knowledge of what we stand for. Those who spend extended amounts of time perfecting their knowledge enhance success through constant efforts. We are not talking about self-indulgence. When we discuss knowing ourselves and knowing others in *The Art of War and Peace*, we are talking about self-evaluation that develops the ability to understand the actions of others.

If frustrations arise, they will only remain temporarily. Driven by the understanding that if I stop now, all progress comes to an end, drives the person to evaluate closer what must be done now to maintain further progress. Understanding ourselves in relation to what we must pursue is essential for establishing the Way. The application of this type of pursuit in knowing ourselves is what will define us. When we begin to develop self-reliance based on what we know and what we can do, our confidence grows.

Never accept anything as common knowledge, lest we forfeit our chance to gain insight into our own reason to act. There is nothing common about life. It is our responsibility to find the Way. When we spend less time blaming others for the misfortune we face, we learn how to overcome them. This is by no means a simple task. This is developed through insight.

This type of thinking must begin with our dedication to effort, or it will be lost to procrastination and laziness.

Indecision renders us incapable of allowing us to think for ourselves. It will accumulate every worthless thought and speculation we can dream of making us incapable of moving forward. What is terrible is a fear of engaging in independent thinking. Because of this, we risk becoming victims of volatile environments that we might encounter. This personal incapability will always be a factor that will decide if we will be happy today or sad tomorrow. Indecisiveness creates a condition of us being prone to failure regardless of our good intentions. We must be able to educate ourselves about the conditions which are required for our success. There is only one way to change the world, and that is by changing how we perceive it.

If you stumble, get up. We have not achieved our destination yet and the longer we remain down, the longer it will take us to continue. We are apprentices and are allowed to stumble, yet we are not allowed to give up. The progress of any action should be considered effective if its outcome brings us closer to success. This allows us to understand the importance of observation and contemplation regarding what must be done next. There is always a correct answer to a question.

Having control of the actions of our body, speech, and mind is essential to bring stability to our life. Uncontrollable desires weaken our abilities to discipline ourselves. Attainment of personal satisfaction is not gained by allowing our sensual wants to overcome our personal needs. What we want and what we need can be a point of conflict.

What we believe in must reflect the direction we have dedicated ourselves to. We must ask ourselves in sincerity what we are dedicated to. If we don't acknowledge to ourselves who we are, the results of what we do will be weakened. Resolve knows no gender, race, or religious affiliation. It is about personal conviction. It is about becoming confident in who we are. There are no specific time tablets that can map out the Way. There are only convictions that will guide us. The Way owes its ability based on multiple factors. The greatest, however, is how we educate ourselves.

The greater the convection, the greater will be the results. The results of such endeavors will be that our path forward will be beyond mistake. Thus, *The Art of War and Peace* states, "The obstacle of forward progress is making mistakes, the solution is, don't make any mistakes." Not making mistakes is the measure of planning we put forth towards our intended goal. If we instill in ourselves the seed of moral clarity, our capability of distinguishing between what is right or wrong, pertinent or irrelevant becomes easier.

Based on our knowledge and investigation, we can simplify our actions into precise science, giving us the capability of grasping what we must do. Simplification is not the process of thinking something is easy. It is more similar to the process of consolidation of information into categories relevant to their problems. This type of effort should encompass every aspect of our lives. Those who live without proper discipline will again and again lose direction and they will never fully understand why they have succeeded or failed in their endeavors. These uninformed people may also face the possibility of becoming prey to those having questionable motivations.

The Rules

When we have developed a template associated with the goals we wish to achieve, we begin to develop discipline. This establishes a verifiable point of growth. Our minds might still wonder and be distracted; however, we will have established the rules we need to aid in structuring our future.

This is not the same thinking that is articulated in the vague expression of "living in the here and now," but a futuristic plan based on what we have today. We engage in the future created by what we are now, and not based on what we wish we were.

Life is not a "do anything you want to do" scenario. When we pass beyond the boundaries of acceptability, we lose direction and squander personal credibility. Those without discipline lose the opportunity of growth beyond their own desires. Any gain they achieve will be temporary and the fear of loss will constantly accompany their thoughts.

In accepting the notion of personal responsibility, we will elevate our worth in the eyes of others. We do not have to follow assumptions that lead us beyond the well-structured plan we have assembled. Therefore, the template we create is there to enhance the goals we set.

Our goals must be directed by understanding that we have the capability to achieve them. How do we know something is achievable? We know because others have also been successful, and if they can do it, then why not me also? Self-confidence propels us beyond what others have thought is impossible.

Being realistic about what we can do at this time is essential. Having patience is a strategy we must employ in all our planning. As stated, we will be capable of doing something only when we are ready. You cannot rush progress or shorten the path to it.

The method of overcoming obstacles is the science of simplifying our investigation of problems. When we understand the nature of a problem, we will begin to comprehend how to solve it. In approaching it in a meticulous manner, we gain personal confidence in our ability to eliminate any obstacle. This way, we start to lose fear and self-doubt. Fear distorts our ability to comprehend what is correct or incorrect. Remember, our intention is to succeed. One of the greatest marks of successful problem solving will be seen in the result of making correct decisions.

The reason for having rules regarding our decision making is to eliminate internal turbulence caused by bad habits. Unrealistic reliance on luck only causes us not to understand that without strategy, the odds of success are not in our favor. We will therefore assume that success is a random occurrence.

We will choose not to rely on scientific investigation to aid us in our life making decisions. In doing so, we open ourselves to exploitation from others because of our lack of preparation and planning. The reality is that in time, we will understand enough to achieve our goals. This is, of course, if we are sincere regarding our reasons for pursuing our goal.

Success is a realistic goal. It springs forth from the thought "I know I can." It is never distracted by the notion of personally having limitations. As mentioned previously, the only limitations we have are the ones we believe in. This is not the same as saying if you believe in something, it will happen. We are saying that based on the law of cause and effect, If we create the correct causes, their results will follow.

Success is not given, and it cannot be bought. It is a result having its own causes that arises from effort and correct actions. Success is not just the result of hard work, education into the laws governing it is also extremely essential. How do we know laws govern it? We know it because this is something that can be reproduced. Success is not the abode of just a chosen few, it belongs to anyone willing to find it. When we find the equation of success our lives change, we begin to know our own potentials. Rules and regulations are the maps given to us to comprehend the route of accomplishment we must take.

Success is not given, it is achieved through understanding and vigilance. Likewise, to be able to maintain our success we must act in the same way. So, this applies with anything we do. The road to understanding success comes in increments and is not miraculously given. Hard work and dedication are necessary, however, correct implementation of actions is the key.

We must employ an internal resolve to continue moving forward, refusing to give up. This means having the ability to research something repeatedly until it becomes an integral part of our understanding. The point of believing that we cannot do something is the point of failure. It is our decision. We must take responsibility upon ourselves; we must believe without hesitation in our own capabilities. Even if others create obstacles that seem insurmountable, if we give up, this is our fault.

There is no such thing as an insurmountable obstacle, there are only temporary ones. The ability to overcome what seems unsurpassable, comes from our contemplation of what is weak and what is strong. As explained previously in *The Art of War and Peace*, by avoiding what is strong and exploiting what is weak, we achieve our goal. Those who spend time in contemplation of these facts will always travel towards success. Those who do not, will be handicapped.

We should abandon all beliefs based on assumption, what we must do is to abandon any action predicating a value on something we have not established as being true. Knowledge comes through investigation. Our capability to investigate is itself an art. Knowledge comes through the door of observation and comparison. It is born through reason and common sense. Our responsibility is to understand its mechanism. If we do not apply our reasoning to reach a verifiable proof, then regardless of our philosophical contentions, we will not be able to come to any valid conclusion regarding what is right or wrong or what actions will bring success or what will not.

We need validation for the purpose of understanding. Many different sciences have been established to facilitate our desire to understand. Here we are referring to the science of grammar, the science of logic, the science of medicine, the science of craftmanship, and the science of the Dharma.[5] When we use these as the foundation of our learning, our understanding can evolve beyond guessing. We must understand that the application of common sense extends beyond just these sciences, it should be applied throughout whatever is important to us.

Speculation or assumption is a mind that does not perceive its desired object. It cannot be trusted as a tool capable of validating what we wish to know. When we say that assumption does not perceive its object, we are stating that it does not understand it. It presumes something to be true but is incapable of establishing its reality.

There are five divisions of assumption: Assumption that has no reason, assumption that has a reason, assumption that has opposing reasons, assumption whose reason has not been ascertained, and assumption that although it has a reason, it has not been established. Assumption conjures a reason without firm evidence. It is an unreliable perception. To be able to understand what something is we must be proficient in validating what we know about it. This is the process of correctly observing the nature of what we seek to know. Our insight should increase from the foundation of what can be proven and not from presumptions. In considering how to deal with any problem, the rule is to never assume. Always proceed cautiously. If we are not certain of the outcome of our actions, remain still.

The principal obstacle maker to our success is caused by mistakes we make in our calculations. The secret to eliminating obstacles is to not make any mistakes. This is not the same as being infallible. We proceed by considering our goal, based on the conditions we must deal with now. We can only

---

5 This correlates to the five major sciences or fields of knowledge in Tibetan Buddhism in which a learned person is supposed to be well versed. The ten sciences (རིག་གནས་བཅུ།) are divided to five major sciences (རིག་གནས་ཆེན་པོ་ལྔ།, namely: craftmanship (བཟོ་རིག་པ།), logic (གཏན་ཚིགས།), grammar (སྒྲ།), medicine (གསོ་བ།), and 'inner science' or Buddhism (ནང་དོན་རིག་པ།) and five minor sciences (རིག་གནས་ཆུང་ལྔ།), namely: synonyms (མངོན་བརྗོད།), mathematics and astrology (སྐར་རྩིས།), performance or drama (ཟློས་གར།), poetry (སྙན་ངག), and composition (སྡེབ་སྦྱོར།).

proceed forward with the capabilities we have now, not with conditions we wish we had. Our action must function within this world we live in.

When we are in doubt about our actions, we must pause until we can validate what will benefit us. The rule is that, if what we are doing brings us a benefit, proceed. If what we are doing does not benefit us, then stop.

When we simplify our rules, they become easy to remember and easy to apply. Be careful not to blame others for our difficulties. There will always be obstacles. The biggest obstacle is the idea of our inability. When we say, "I cannot," the possibility of further progress stops.

Most problems hindering our progress come from our lack of diligence. Many opportunities are missed because of losing sight of what must be done. This happens because we lose patience with our own speed of progress. As pointed out previously, we should formulate a template of success. Rules are essential. We should divide our goals into two divisions: long-term, and short-term. In this case we will define long-term as goals that will be completed in one year or greater and short-term goals are goals that can be completed in less than that.

This method allows us to understand the sequence of priorities. Fluency in our abilities comes from meticulous attention to detail. We cannot rush success, success comes in increments. The reality is that it is impossible to digest information faster than we are capable of comprehending. The world we live in is complex and the interdependent nature of things is not always obvious. The saying "Rome was not built in a day" is not a slogan, it is an insight.

Our engagement in any new endeavor should be considered as an apprenticeship. Those with little knowledge who proclaim mastery are foolish. Build a solid foundation using short-term goals to master long-term success. We must devote our time in planning and this planning should be submerged in correct reasoning. Make no mistakes.

There is no such thing as an ability to predict the future. We should give up all reliance on horoscopes, soothsayers, or any unproven method of divining the potential future of success or failure. The interdependent nature of existence offers only a snapshot of what might happen but does not supply a complete narrative to the whole story. What we imagine to be true is not always as we believed it to be. Therefore, here comes the need for meticulous investigation. We are capable of coming to valid conclusions. It is our contention that for something to be real, it must depend on it being something that is able to be unmistakably understood. If that is not possible then the belief is fake.

Scientific investigation depends on the ability to reproduce the experiment over and over again. Inconsistent results introduce a possibility of chance and should never reside in the realm of scientific discussion. Future events deduced by divination cannot be examined for their validity, so it is advised to not rely upon them. It is not my intention to say some divinations are not true. I am saying that if you know how to achieve your objective, why would you need divination? Study well the content of this writing.

The rules and methods explained here are not only based on the law of interdependency but also on the law of cause and effect. We must understand that we live in a world governed by conditions. Wisdom seeks to understand the relationship of things without any participation in assumption. In Buddhist theology these relationships are extensively explained in many scriptural treaties.

How we decide to address our obstacles will determine whether we will succeed or fail. Without determining our direction at this time, the path to the desired future becomes endangered. Therefore, the values we nurture today are important. Not everyone needs to follow these instructions, but for those who are not satisfied with unpredictable accomplishments, these rules are essential. Long-term sustainability of our action is not something that can be accomplished when we have no rules to govern ourselves.

The foundation for gaining success is based on our own determination and belief that *I can do*. We should rid our vocabulary of words like, I cannot, it will not, it is not possible and so on. There are many sources of doubt that by force of habit invade our personalities limiting our capability. If we say I cannot, then further progress comes to an end. The seeds of progress spring forth from the internal spirit of optimism. If we fail, it is because we stopped trying. We are not saying to repeat the same actions that previously failed over and over again, we are saying find another route. We can overcome our difficulties by adapting our actions to the problems at hand. Failure is only a temporary condition. It is not an indication of the outcome of our goal. If the resolution takes time, so be it.

A superior person clearly understands that we are in the constant grip of change. Just as water takes the shape of the land it traverses, so must we also shape our strategies in accordance with the realities we encounter.

Self-confidence is essential for our ability to proceed forward. Therefore, it is necessary to continuously renew our source of insight in relation to what is factual and what is not.

There should come a point in our learning when knowledge transcends the written word into the realm of understanding. We should not form our comprehension based on what has been passed on to us by others. This is not insight, this is mere mimicking. Insight can be understood by seeing the resulting solution through research and coming to subsequent conclusions.

Understanding is attained through the process of becoming acquainted with information. This is a cornerstone of insight. The process of understanding is enhanced through our ability to simplify information surrounding the challenge we are facing. This process allows us to focus without distraction on the source of our dilemma. It seems that people whom we consider ahead of the curb are those who are constantly reviewing what they know or contemplating on different approaches to their situations.

The method of simplifying a problem is accomplished by meticulous and detailed research into the challenge. We must focus on a subject, express what we are predicating about it and then establish a valid reason supporting our justification.[6] If what we believe in does not convey a viable explanation and a justification, then it lacks the quality of being an answer.

Once again, there is no fast lane in researching the information which will lead us to a correct decision. What is essential for us is to become comfortable with the disciplines required in attaining our aspirations. Sun Tzu in *The Art of War* explains, "The superior generals are those who spend a long time in their temple contemplating the outcome of their battle." When we contemplate the correctness of our actions, we should understand that the only thing that separates our actions from the art of war is the motivation we possess. Therefore we should understand that as it is in war, so is it in peace.

The first step to understanding "how" is the step of educating ourselves. Since logic combines correct rationale and observation, it can be identified as a science. Logic is important in deciphering the nature of things that are not empirically evident. Each step taken to formulate a correct understanding builds a valid hypothesis, which is important to understanding. The rules are explained in the text, Pramanavartika (Tib. Tsema Namdrel)[7]. There are also other commentaries that can be referenced regarding the subject of valid cognition.

Simplification of a problem depends on our ability to focus on the subject which is being evaluated. We all have a learning capability. Some people learn some things faster than others and some have greater retention abilities; however, the process needed to understand a subject remains the same. We should not hinder our learning ability by introducing ourselves to notions of incapability.

The problem of not being able to learn something is usually caused by our lack of applying our mind to the subject. There are many reasons why absence of attention may exist. Lack of preparation can happen because of laziness, personal distractions or just because we have never been taught the

---

6　This method follows Tibetan discipline of debates, which trains the students in focusing on the subject, predicate, and reason (ཆོས་ཅན། གསལ་བ། རྟགས།) without being distracted by opinions or other topics.

7　By Pramāṇavārtika (Skt.) or ཚད་མ་རྣམ་འགྲེལ། (Tib.) is influential work on logic by Dharmakīrti (Skt.) or ཆོས་ཀྱི་གྲགས་པ། (Tib.) – a great 6th or 7th century Nālandā scholar.

proper methods to learn. If we understand our own potential, then we will never limit ourselves to what others may have deemed as being insurmountable. Learning is the process of sharpening our personal skills.

Preparation is essential. A superior person spends a long time contemplating what is necessary for them to go forward. The superior person educates themselves in all facets of what has to be done. If, for example, we have a test in three months, now is the time to begin our preparations. This is the method of understanding the topic through repetition. When we are not under stress, every day, we should familiarize ourselves with our subject of study. In this way there will be no surprises.

Shantideva stated: "There is nothing that does not become easier through repetition." Through the discipline of constantly renewing our understanding of the subject, we will eventually become well acquainted with its topic. The consequences of being uninformed afflicts those lacking preparation; not planning for the future is foolish. The notion that I can learn anything is conditional. The condition for understanding must be realized through repetitive effort in understanding the subject. Do not fear or become discouraged by having to review a topic over and over again.

The purpose of words is to communicate the meaning an author wished to express. Communication is a process of making a subject comprehensible to all. Words are here to make the intended meaning visible; they are meant to bring unmistakable clarity. Any comment other than a direct or indirect intended statement of the author is a commentary. A commentary is an expression of somebody else's comprehension, and it may or may not reflect the real intention of the original author.

In Tibetan script, we would be talking about the root text of an author and commentaries made by others. This points out the obligation to constantly review our understanding of what we wish to know. Not all scholastic commentaries are correct interpretations; they must also be validated.

The initial process of learning is an apprenticeship, which refers to the time spent developing our understanding of what is needed to master our skills. During this time, mastery is not the primary focus. We must first train and sharpen our ability to be able to correctly implement whatever we need to know to achieve it. The more we become accustomed to the disciplines of our task, the further we will be capable to advance our agenda. Therefore, plan your time well. Those who reach the mastery of their skills are those who advance their understanding of what forms the structures of their aspirations.

The main hinderances to our achievements are laziness and self-imposed limitations. When we choose to believe that we cannot do something, all forward progress halts. If we are climbing a great mountain and we conclude halfway up, "I cannot do this," all possibilities of attaining the summit are lost. We will go no further because we have decided this fate for ourselves.

Finding a scapegoat by blaming others is a shameless act of denying personal responsibility.

Unrealistic expectations do not serve us during any part of our journey. If everything we do must be completed now, maybe our anticipations exceed reality. Meticulous attention to time and effort tumbles all obstacles.

$$S = (A+ CF) > P$$

Solution equals the application of continuous force greater than the problem.

I did not say an overwhelming force. This is because continuous force becomes eventually overwhelming. We create an opportunity by cultivating our own skills and capabilities. The more time we spend doing what we wish to master, the better we get. We excel beyond expectations when we understand that we can always do something better. We should understand that there are levels of comprehension as there are also different levels of experts and different levels of insight.

We should never hinder our progress by accepting blindly that someone else may have a deeper insight into a subject because of the notoriety, name, or title. If we do so, we limit our ability to be inquisitive. Our path does not become clear if we cannot explain logically why we think as we do.

The problem of having to express the notion that you believe in something because your teacher says so, is a weak position to take. This becomes apparent when someone else does not accept your teacher as a valid point or reference. Therefore, regardless of the respect we might personally have for the source of our knowledge, we must strive to achieve an understanding based on our own personal investigation.

What happens when we investigate? We eliminate doubt. Doubt is what places us in the state of turmoil, it presents us as incapable, and it causes us to lack the confidence about what we have to do. Confidence is essential. Confidence radiates personal achievements that have made differences in our lives.

In our social surroundings we are not taught how to gain confidence. Usually we are taught conformity and obedience. We are constantly under the scrutiny of those who wish to define who we are. This is not acceptable. When we decide not to follow cultural standards, initially some level of fear arises. This is because we personally become responsible for what happens to ourselves. Let morality be our guide. The strongest people in the world are those who carry moral responsibility as the cornerstone of all they do. Moral responsibility begins with commitment to the rules concerning our actions of body, speech, and mind.

When we suggest moral commitment as the foundation of building character, we are clearly aware that there are people without moral devotion who become successful without including ethics in their everyday lives. However, this is not the rule, and we are not trying to secure short-term benefits. When the outcome of our success does not acknowledge our reliance on others, our actions become short sighted, and we can become cruel and isolated. When the only thing our authority is focused on is personal benefit by suppression of others, we have not become a true leader.

Through this discussion we are building success for the purpose of prolonged benefit to all. There will be obstacles, this is the nature of things that transit from one point to another. Yet, obstacles do not hinder us as long as our shared goals are similar. Barriers only become insurmountable when we have mentally constructed a reason for them to exist. There are always solutions to problems. When we have learned to evaluate our progress from a different point of view and to see obstacles as mere challenges, we are in the position to find an adequate solution. When we look at every obstacle as an opportunity, our world changes and we are no longer enslaved by our doubts.

Being strong does not eliminate being compassionate. Being compassionate does not equate with being subservient and being subservient is not a measure of humbleness.

The world is complex, but that does not mean it is not manageable. Our personal actions are no more complicated than anyone else's. Therefore, know oneself and know others. In *The Art of War* Sun Tzu clearly emphasizes the requirement of this type of investigation. If we apply efforts in knowing ourselves and knowing others, we will be always successful. Knowing means we will understand how to apply our actions to all situations as they arise. As stated, if you understand oneself but not others, we will be victorious fifty percent of the time; if we understand both ourselves and others, we will never see defeat.

Ideology

Ideology is a science of ideas. We must contemplate well its meaning. When we understand its nature, we begin to recognize the importance of this word. Words are crucial keys to understanding the significance of a given advice.

Bonds among people are cemented by shared beliefs, these shared beliefs are what define us as a people, as a group, or as a nation and determines the success or failure of any organization. The more people see shared experiences in terms of ideas they believe in, the stronger the bond will grow. Civilizations rise based on principles they have in common and fall when these principles lose their meaning. When new ideologies spring forth, the society begins to change.

Of course, there can be contributing conditions, however, the principal factors come from within. These factors can be measured, and we should be cognitive of different variants that favor or not our principles. Ideology displays the depth of belief we may be willing to sacrifice ourselves for. The strength of truth we see in these ideas will determine our dedication.

Imposing our assumptions on others regarding their capabilities blurs our capacity to understand who we are dealing with. Knowing only ourselves means we are not open to investigating there is a possibility we have underestimated others. In this case we believe only in the superiority of our own self-believed contentions without exploring what others may really think.

This is a recipe for disaster, however, we see this happen again and again. It is human nature to overestimate self-importance, which invites uncertain consequences. Before venturing forward, contemplate in earnest both our ideology and those of others. In doing so we will begin to know how to propagate our own.

Wealth and military strength do not constitute true power, ideology does.

Avoidance of Strong, Exploitation of Weak

Here we are talking about making our efforts successful. We advance ourselves by understanding strong factors that favor our rivals and weak factors that favor us. The formula instructs us to avoid the strong and exploit the weak. By doing so, our competitors will constantly be forced to react defensively to whatever we do.

If they are many and we are a few, we must force them to divide their capabilities. If they are rich and we are poor, we must make them have great expenditures. When they are forced to divide their energy and we remain as one, we become the strong and they become the weaker.

We must avoid conditions that will bring us loss or no beneficial results at all. When obstacles greater than our capabilities arise, we must avoid direct contact by finding other remedies that will allow us to continue forward. Finding other remedies is not retreat, it is just a strategic maneuver to distract others from our actual intentions.

To exhaust our efforts on things that will bring little or no benefit is likened to us winning a battle but losing the war. When others are strong and we directly engage them, we are playing a fool's game. If a direct confrontation does not improve our status, we must look for an alternative means of continuing our progress.

Remember, $S = (A+CF) > P$, *solution equals the application of continuous force greater than the problem.* Success must grow from the combination of strategy and continuous effort. Continuous effort brings mastery when we believe in what we do.

Application of a continuous force is always maintaining our efforts towards our intended goal. This is the process of not giving up. If we take off to a long journey and upon reaching halfway give up, we will never reach our desired destination. When we lose determination, we have given up on our future progress.

Never shy away from conflict. We must and should remember there is always conflict surrounding us. Forces are always in opposition to what we wish to achieve. Having opposition should have no consequence to us and what we do. We must just adjust our strategy and continue moving forward.

The Method

Initially it is not always clear what we must do when we first engage in an action we have not done before. It is important to understand the concept of insight through education. The actions we participate in the present are an indication of what we will achieve later. Each action we achieve towards our goal should be seen as a steppingstone to that successful outcome.

We must not be ignorant of the relationship between what we are doing now and what we will perfect through time. Be aware of the precondition of having patience with ourselves and maintain dedication to our goal.

There are great differences between those who succeed and those who fail. We must understand that there is a definable distinction regarding their commitment to preparation. For those who do not believe in strategy confusion arises, while those who prepare approach their challenges with clarity.

The chaos factor is a belief that success happens randomly. This belief says that what happens to us is controlled externally by forces beyond our possible comprehension. This type of belief, to varying degree, is prolific among the majority of people. The chaos factor is just a belief; however, it can control every level of self-confidence. Indecision or self-doubt will dominate our judgments and we will rely more and more on divinations or some other systems of chance in making choices.

Overcoming these types of obstructions lies in our ability to identify, investigate, and eliminate what hinders our progress. These are not isolated and standalone conditions; these are conditions that vary in their potential to limit our capability to identify what exactly is the problem.

We must conclude prior to any engagement the reality of our own responsibility to achieve success. If we don't have clarity, we will not be able to instill the respect that we need to be identified as a leader. Success and leadership share the same throne.

We are not describing leadership by attrition; we are talking about leadership based on personal moral qualities. We are describing leadership that springs forth from individual dedication to the purpose.

We must realistically distinguish our goals from our wants. Impatience can also become a great hinderance in decision making. Impatience hinders our ability to separate what we want to happen and what we need to do. It distorts our ability to illuminate what should be done.

Why do We Need Theory

Theory gives direction to the meaning of our beliefs. This guides us to a course of determining what we will or will not accept. Those who do not have theory are weakened. They are not able to project leadership for themselves or others. Lack of direction will produce only a measured or limited amount of success.

Success of any group of people depends on having a cohesive agreement that unify their capabilities to work together. The stronger the unity, the more successful the group will be. If we use only one straw of a broom to sweep a floor, we achieve limited success, however, when bundled with many other strands, our work become more effective.

There must be a traceable and mutually accepted foundation for everyone to rally around. Although personalities offer a point of devotion, they will only function well when that particular personality is present. It is *sine qua non* to make the beliefs of an organization clear to all who show interest.

This type of thought doesn't equate with being subservient to a master. It means that all participants have a choice. If a person doesn't like the rules of the group, they should be able to leave. Not everyone will carry the same motivations. By making the rules clear, we can distinguish between those who will be dedicated and those will not commit themselves.

Commitment is not difficult to understand. Individual leadership can start at any level, and those who believe in the process will excel. Those who lack dedication will show contempt for the rules, they will be lazy, and their participation will be short. There is no real reason to keep those of weak conviction. They eventually become a burden to the group requiring greater and greater attention, thus hindering all potential growth.

If a person believes in the philosophy of a group, then it's their responsibility to learn as much as possible about it. In this way, personal status will grow. True leadership develops from taking on individual responsibility and performing duties as if they were central to the function of that organization.

The reality is that all organizations survive because of the dedication of its people. Leadership relies on efforts from those who support the groups' view. The more we are committed to benefiting the organization, the better we will be able to merge all aspects of a group.

All problems are solvable. We must face our challenges through realistic planning. This should be understood by evaluating what is possible and what is not. Sometimes part of the solution involves just time and patience. This allows us to navigate our action in a way that finds what is best for us.

We don't have to know everything. We must be willing to learn what we must know. Especially during our time when information can be received easily, just using our keyboard can supplement learning.

We should learn how to prioritize what is most important to our future by comprehending the causal factors of now. This is done through planning. There are oceans of information for us to consider.

There should be clarity in our minds when we interact with others. We must understand clearly that compromise and appeasement are not the same thing. Compromising is a method of negotiating disputes bringing benefit to both sides. This means we get something out of the deal. Appeasement is the policy of acceding to the demands of a potentially hostile entity in the hope of maintaining peace. The problem with this is that the root of the trouble will never be extinguished, and transgressions will continue again and again.

Common sense is the foundation of good decision making. Of course, we must understand there are instructions on how to do things. As explained before, this is what apprenticeship is about. However, common sense is king. When looking at a puzzle, the pieces must come together based on basic rules. There are no magical routes to a successful outcome of what we plan to do. Elaborate speculation regarding how something should be done has less importance in us coming to a decision than just asking ourselves if that make sense.

Simplification of something complex adheres to the advice of applying common sense to what we do. We must always ask ourselves, does what we have investigated provide a remedy to problems or does it not. Does the solution create more questions than answers?

If our answers are vague, then we have not researched an adequate to answer our question. Life only becomes more complicated when we allow our thinking to be unclear. Therefore, clarity should spring forth not only from what we study but also from our ability to think. Learning is our responsibility.

A Matter of Choice

There are many variants our discussion can branch into, but the subject of creating stability within our own lives must be the most essential factor we should contemplate. Stability comes from balancing our needs with our wants. Needs should be understood here as indispensable requirements in supporting ourselves. Wants extend themselves beyond things we require. They can be understood as tendencies lacking satisfaction. Lack of satisfaction can arise because of habit or because of social factors but in any case, it should be understood as a personal choice.

We are in the situations we experience because of selections we make. To succeed or to fail is created by our choices. We must educate ourselves thoroughly. We must allow ourselves to experience the right choices in life if we wish to be successful and if we wish to be happy.

The world we live in reflects the choices we have made. The affect we have on others can be far reaching. The extent of our influence upon others can also be beneficial or devastating. Having good intentions is not enough. Just because we hold good thoughts, this does not guarantee a successful outcome to our work. If we examine the decisions of successful people, we will start to be aware of how to conduct ourselves.

There is a question asking: "Does society corrupt man or does man corrupt society?" Regardless of the conditions we are born in, we must understand our future is determined by our own decisions. We have the choice. Poverty or wealth does not determine who we are or what we can do.

When dealing with others, always be aware of their potential to generate deception. When engaging in any endeavor, always ponder who will benefit from our participation. The trick of deception is making others believe what is not true, to be true or what is true, to be false. We are not saying not to trust anyone; we are saying it is necessary to maintain caution.

There are many variations of deception, however the variants are similar. Even if we are right, the objective of deception is to promote doubt in our own personal decisions. If what is being displayed doesn't make sense, then approach it with skepticism. For those who do not use their common sense and determine their forward progress based on blind trust, loss will follow.

When we are able to identify the intentions of others, when we are able to characterize the source of confusion, our ability to navigate the obstacles in front of us and conduct ourselves in proper actions becomes second nature.

Gaslighting tries to present us in the light of how someone else wants to define us to be and not as we are. This misrepresentation can be spread through rumor, group pressure or by our wish to belong. If we lose our personal confidence, we compromise who we are. If we allow our self-worth to diminish, we will eventually be left with nothing. Therefore, never speak or think bad of oneself even in jest.

Know yourself and then know others. Bullying is a constant pressure experienced by many regardless of their age. Conditions of degradation will be interrupted by short moments of praise giving hope of acceptance. This however will be short lived. If we feel overwhelmed, then leave the abusive situation.

The world will continue to spin. The point is the imperative of using and believing in our own common sense. If we believe ourselves to be partially to blame for someone else's aggression and don't recognize ourselves as victims, we will lose our future.

Building Wealth

Building wealth is more than just the physical possession of items of value. Wealth implies the mental attitude we bring with us in confronting the challenges of this life. If we incorporate the philosophy of when during the time of plenty, we save for times of want, we bring stability in our lives.

You cannot segregate our lives from the fact that we need to do something to maintain it. The reality is, not everyone is born with a silver spoon in their mouths but that should not be a deterrent to living our lives in accordance with what we wish to do. Wealth should also be something we internalize.

If our utilization of wealth is based on what others describe to us as normal, we will always be in want. When wealth becomes the obsession built on the concept of "whoever dies with the most toys, wins," we will never achieve satisfaction, we will never obtain what is best for us.

Regardless of what type of society we live in, the challenge of personal stability is our own responsibility. The biggest problem is that we lack instruction on how we succeed in the environments we live in. The reality is that people who are successful through their own mental attitude will be successful regardless of their geographical location.

Opportunity is not governed by geography, race, religion, or cultural differences. It comes from mentally being able to frame our future. We are often taught that circumstances control our future but within the framework of Buddhist understanding, we control our destiny because it is us who make the decisions. Freedom or bondage is determined by what we are willing to accept. What distinguishes the bad from the good depends on the nature of our motivation.

The same nature of physics that govern those who have something governs those who have nothing. Therefore, there is a sort of equality that governs us all. The obstacles of life may vary but the methods of approaching them are similar. We must allow ourselves time to consider other avenues to success.

We will always find that our abilities to do something are governed by three types of powers. The first is overwhelming power, the second is equal power, and the third is inferior power. These are only indication of present strength and by no means are decisive to any outcome. These are only conditions we must deal with, and we must be aware of the abilities of others in relation to our own. As stated before, wealth comes from internal abilities and not because of physical strength. Size matters but strategy dominates.

The basic rules are: When we have overwhelming power, continue forward, when we have equal power, proceed with caution, and maneuver when our advantage is weak. In this case, we must evaluate their strengths and weaknesses. Conditions regarding engagements are always changing. When we understand this, we will be capable of timing our actions benefiting our intentions.

The physics regarding application is universally the same regardless of individual motivations. No matter if we are a good person or a bad person, the equation 1+1 will always equal 2, no matter what universe we decide to live in.

Success is ornamented by our motivation, but our intentions do not dictate an outcome. Motivation creates who we are and what we have become. This explanation goes well with understanding our notion of Buddhist physics. Buddhist physics encompasses both wisdom and method.

Wealth is a product of how we live, and we have the opportunity to participate in having it. The point is that its achievability is universally there. Wealth or poverty is the house we decide to live in and reflects the choices we have made or are making in life.

Common sense is not difficult, it is not rocket science. It is merely something we have not relied on. Independent thinking sometimes makes others uneasy because it considers acts beyond convention. We will be told that our ideas are not correct, and we will be advised of more traditional manners of thinking. This is not an indication of the absence of validity of our philosophy; it is an indication of what they cannot understand.

The first and most essential measure of success is when we learn how to be frugal with what we have now. Having a long-term understanding will affect our future. Short term planning leaves no room for times of need.

Educate ourselves, understand the actions of those who have been successful, develop bonds with others you can trust and always expand knowledge beyond the subjects explained in this book.

Insight Through Education

Insight through education refers to the relationship between practice and education. It is a cornerstone that will lead us to success and distinguish us from others.

We are always trying our best to find ways to achieve our desires. To accomplish this, we are required to set forth viable philosophies helping us to accomplish our goals. Wishing for something is no more than an indication of the direction we want to go in. Achieving that wish requires a structure – a viable plan must be an essential part of our strategy. The result of following the template is that it can be reproduced again and again.

If we have a plan, and if we have a goal, but we do not take the time to explore how we should follow it, we put ourselves in the position of uncertainty regarding what we should or should not do. This brings forth the necessity of the philosophy that will determine us. (Every philosophy must be rooted in common sense.) When we say philosophy, we are talking about it in terms of viability. Being viable brings an understanding that it is functional.

We should be as true to our philosophy as we are to our goal. Whenever we do not mutually support each other, we will find that our objective will not be reached, nor it will be understood. The function of philosophy is to bring clarity. Clarity springs forth from how we educate ourselves.

Our slogan *insight through education* highlights the importance of study. It has become clear to us that there is confusion regarding learning. The source of knowledge in essence comes from the interaction between the teacher, their understanding of the material at hand, the presentation of that information, and the personal comprehension we gain from this type of interaction. This is what we consider as insight.

Therefore, learning becomes the responsibility of students to engage in the process of thinking and not merely absorbing the information. To be able to parrot information without utilizing the process of reasoning brings detriment to one's ability to transform intellectual information into personal insight.

Our own personal value should be measured by the value we are able to bring to others. If our goals are to benefit and change the society in which we want to live in, our pursuit of excellence should be well established in knowledge, which is not merely accumulated from others, but we have also determined it to be true.

About the Author

Geshe Jampa Kunchog is an American Buddhist monk who has studied in Sera Jey Monastic University for over twenty years and then also taught there. He is a student of the well-known Sera Jey Geshe, Geshe Ngawang Dhargey.

Upon finishing his studies and returning to the West, Geshe Jampa established the Scholastic Institute Chokyi Gyaltsen (SICGU). The goal of SICGU is to promote and preserve Tibetan Buddhism as it has been traditionally taught for hundreds of years in the Tibetan lineage. The background in Western culture as well as in the formal Buddhist training, gives Geshe la a very unique combination of scholarly knowledge and practical advice.

Since the inception of SICGU, Geshe la Jampa Kunchog has been giving teachings on general Buddhism, Tibetan language and grammar and traditional philosophical studies as taught to the monks at Sera Jey Monastic University. He is also leading the translating and publishing activities of SICGU Dhargey Publishing.

Today he continues to give teachings and offer advice to his students with great kindness and patience.

About SICGU

Scholastic Institute Chokyi Gyaltsen (SICGU, pronounce *see-gyu*) was established in 1995 to facilitate the growing interest in traditional Tibetan philosophy and culture in the West. Our goal is to provide to our communities accurate and authentic information on Tibetan Buddhist philosophy, traditional Tibetan medicine, and classical Tibetan art. Additionally, through the usage of technology and publication, we are able to offer similar services to the national and international community online.

The goal of SICGU is to develop a university that will provide outstanding teachers in this tradition as well as extensive resources, focused on the idea that through research comes knowledge, from knowledge comes practice, and from practice come realizations.

During the transfer of Buddhism to Tibet, Tibetan monks traveled to India, studied with the great scholars of the day, and became experts in Sanskrit. Similarly to what happened over a thousand years ago, we are faced with the responsibility of disseminating the teachings in the West now. SICGU aims at producing new generations of scholars to examine the validity of Buddhist physics.

Scholastic Institute Chokyi Gyaltsen (SICGU) is dedicated to preservation and dissemination of Tibetan Buddhist study and meditation in accordance to the Nalanda tradition, following the advice of His Holiness Dalai Lama and the lineage of Sera Jey Monastic University. We are providing scriptural commentaries expounding the intended meaning of the Buddha's doctrine and teachings on this vast and difficult to understand philosophy.

Our highly qualified teachers, both Tibetan and Western Geshes, are offering classes in Tibetan language, philosophy, and logic. We are offering you the opportunity to understand deeper the practice of Tibetan Buddhist lineage and to procure a certificate or, through time, the degree in Buddhist studies.

Our study program assists the needs of all who are interested in attaining comprehensive insight into the teachings and who want to learn how to debate and engage in various related discourses.

SICGU's aim is to provide learning that will be second to none. Our main resource of teachers comes from Sera Jey University in India. They provide serious students a complete insight into the wisdom of this tradition. Based on the commentary of the Great Tibetan scholars, Je Rinpoche Lobsang Drakpa, Gyaltsab Je, Khedup Je and the great Jetsun Chokyi Gyaltsen, it is our intention to build a university as a door of understanding these precious teachings.

We offer you the opportunity to see how we distinguish ourselves from other organizations. The difference is not something that can be understood in terms of dollars and cents, but by our method of thinking and how we understand what is necessary to become a practitioner. The relationship between practice and education is a cornerstone that will distinguish us from others.

The most important thing for us now is to open a dialogue about the future of Buddhism in the west and the future of Buddhism in our personal practices. Both will be essential for establishment of Buddhism in the west.

$$(TC) PS = S + T > IC$$

At the time of the cause, the probability of success equals the strength and time invested in the task being greater to the intended completion.

About SICGU Dhargey Publishing

SICGU Dhargey Publishing is the publishing branch of SICGU.

The primary purpose of SICGU Dhargey Publishing is to make Tibetan Buddhist scholarly material available to western students. We also strive to present a wide range of materials related to Tibetan culture and Buddhism.

SICGU Dhargey Publishing presents translations of classical texts of the Tibetan Buddhist tradition, focused primarily on study material utilized by students following the Geshe program at Sera Jey Monastic University, thus making this important material available to English-speaking students for the first time. All of our study materials are bi-lingual, Tibetan-English, thus offering students an opportunity to work with both vocabularies at once.

An important focus of SICGU Dhargey Publishing is classical Tibetan language and grammar. We are preparing Tibetan-English translations of the main Tibetan grammatical literature to support and encourage precise translations of canonical literature. Another priority of SICGU Dhargey Publishing is presenting the essential teachings of the Buddha Dharma in a manner accessible to contemporary students.

SICGU Dhargey Publishing plans to publish biographical, historical, and cultural works as well other materials relevant to our mission. We are also a publisher of children's books that present the timeless values of Buddhist philosophy, making them accessible to readers of all levels.

Purchasing titles from SICGU Dhargey Publishing supports our mission and will help us to publish, distribute and preserve these important treasures of Tibetan Buddhist scholarship for generations to come.

www.ingramcontent.com/pod-product-compliance
Lightning Source LLC
Chambersburg PA
CBHW070210100426
42743CB00013B/3120